AF248860

FILMING ASSASSINATIONS

Work on this collection and the poems in it was supported in part by grants from the National Endowment for the Arts, the Research Foundation of the State University of New York, and the New York State Council on the Arts' Creative Arts Public Service Programs.

FILMING ASSASSINATIONS

Poems by

DAVE KELLY

ITHACA HOUSE

Acknowledgements

The Paris Review, LaHuerta, Atlantic Monthly, Runcible Spoon, The Back Door, Striver's Row, Aisling, Ark River Review, New Letters, Quarry, Choice, Out Of This World: Poems from the Hawkeye State, Capstan, Westigan Review, Bartleby's Review, The Iowa Review, The Wormwood Review, California Quarterly, Poetry Texas, Poet Lore, Sotto Voce, New Generation of Poetry, Ann Arbor Review, Poetry Now, Lillabulero, Unmuzzled Ox, Occident, The Red Clay Reader, Bartholomew's Cobble, Hearse.

The publication of this book has been made possible with public funds from the New York State Council on the Arts.

ITHACA HOUSE, 108 N. Plain St., Ithaca, NY 14850

Distributed by SBD, 1636 Ocean View Ave. Kensington, CA 94707

Library of Congress Cataloging in Publication Data

Kelly, Dave, 1938-
    Filming assassinations.

    I. Title.
PS3561.E39314F54   811'.5'4   79-17783
ISBN 0-87886-106-8

For Sylvia

Books and chapbooks by Dave Kelly:

THE NIGHT OF THE TERRIBLE LADDERS, Hors
Commerce Press, 1966
DEAR NATE, Runcible Spoon Press, 1969
SUMMER STUDY, Runcible Spoon Press, 1969
ALL HERE TOGETHER, Lillabulero Press, 1969
INSTRUCTIONS FOR VIEWING A SOLAR
ECLIPSE, Wesleyan University Press, 1972
AT A TIME: A DANCE FOR VOICES, Basilisk
Press, 1972
DID YOU HEAR THEY'RE BEHEADING BILL
JOHNSON TODAY?, The Stone Press, 1974
THE FLESH EATING HORSE AND OTHER SAGAS,
Bartholomew's Cobble Press, 1976
IN THESE ROOMS, Red Hill Press, 1976
POEMS IN SEASON, Texas Portfolio Press, 1977

CONTENTS

THIS PLACE

Someone is in my room, reading my poems.
I feel the chill along my backbone as his finger
shirrs the tops of the pages, as his thumb
digs into a place between two stanzas.

My teeth grind in my sleep as he laughs
at a line I meant to be wept over, as he skips
a whole poem, as his mind underlines

a section I had meant to remove, a section
in which I make a desperate confession
and a section in which I fear my own death. His
eyes run so lightly over my tombstones

that I don't even have time to die under them
that I wouldn't die if I dared or wanted
to, this son of a bitch with his hands and eyes

in my parents, in the losses of my friends
with his boredom riding over all my apologies
and his presence like a cat burglar in my poems
and in my poor sleep two doors down this hall.

Today there is only
this place with me

in it, this room
on a lake I have
seen before.

For three days the
water has been

freezing.

It is not solid yet.

There are still
puddles of water
breaking through

all the way across.
The fish I

suppose breathe
through them

claustrophobia
squeezing around
their minds

and the birds
still feed
through the holes.

I go to town
twice each day
buying things we

need, food and
magazines, the

morning paper. Levels
of the hill
across the lake

are packed with
depths of snow.

They make shades
of white and brown
along themselves.

If the children
get the habit of

walking on ice
this winter we

will have to
break them of it

when spring comes.

1

In the middle of the Detroit River
the monster Zug Island devours the workers
behind its iron fences while the earth

moves around the sun, imploding gases
in its wake and filling convertibles
with the soft woolen hips of nymphomaniacs.

My father shows his photograph to the guard
on the midnight shift and disappears
forever into the jaws of light. I sit in the car

with the motor running and watch him. Tomorrow
when I go downstairs late and pass his door I'll
wonder at the strange head on the pillow inside.

2

Two kids
coming
out of school
said

let's go
down
to the dump
tonight

kill rats
in the
pale
car lights

and stop
after that
at dumb
Jeannie's house

and their
voices
trailed
out of sight.

3

Our hands fit into each other.
The car breaks through the night.
Inside it is warm and we don't speak.

I have just seen your head broken
your eyes open under the right front bumper.
I know what your blood will look like

and the wheel spinning
in the air above you

(I have lain in the middle of that scene
myself, waiting for the hands to come
and lift the metal from my chest)

and that some day you will leave me
that way or any other.

4

Now these are the men with the empire
in their tremendous laps: one bites off
chunks of painted steel and swallows
them without chewing; one chomps down
a semi filled with whitewall tires; the
third drinks tankers full of crude oil.
They eye your skinny legs for toothpicks.

5

Her hips, naked,
rest in the
large hands
of the basketball star.

He turns her
in his curled fists
and her
eyes are closed.

The onions on his
damp breath,
radio singing behind
her thin back

she is too young
to be beautiful
but her long hair
and the length of
her sighing body

bring her here
the queen of
any Friday's
parked convertibles.

6

When the union

leader wants
to show

his men why he can run things

better
from a cell

than most men in an office he

still
calls

in a photographer and rolls up

his blue-and-white

striped
shirt, the

thirty-year
old

bullet scar

still worth a thousand votes

and
every cent he's stolen.

7

It was the week of burning cities.
Firemen lay on the asphalt, the eyes
of snipers buried in their backs.

Governors were calling for help
and farm boys drove to town
with shotguns in the backseats

of their Fords. It was also the week
the baby was constipated, the dead fish
lined the great lake and the water

was too cold for swimming.
I drove into the city with Gary
to rescue two old ladies from

god knew what in the streets
and they compared the sizes
of each other's butcher knives.

One wore every jewel she owned
to save them from black rapists,
the other's jaw shook all the way

home. Shopkeepers were boarding their
windows as we drove out. One, a blonde,
wrote Soul Brother on his boards.

8

Carl stands in a shady corner of the porch
and rolls his Bull Durham into a twist with
one hand as he tells us about the marines
and the war. We don't notice his hand at the
edges of Susan's dress. His voice thick and
rusty. I'm so scared of the Japs he creates
and kills with his story I have to pee. We
take Hill 107 together. Carl in command. Me.
Billy. Susan is our nurse. For the wounded.
With his scratchy hand crawling under her
skirt. It's been there all summer but we
haven't noticed. She's been less eager to
go there every morning and she cries now,
sometimes, at supper without saying why. The
mortars are burning in shells at us now. A
Jap screams, "Banzai!" We take cover long
enough to catch our breath. Carl lights his
handrolled cigarette. The birds in her
eyes are caught behind a window's screen.
She starts to move but a hand catches the
back of her neck. The birds die. Susan sits

still. I see and trade her for our summer war.

9

A deer stops on the median outside Lansing
in a smear of headlights too late for brakes

or fear. The silence roars in the ditch
we both come home to. Hours later the sun
creases a hill and finds us both strapped

like autumn to the fenders of a state police car
eyes opened, apples plugged forever in our mouths.

I am sitting on a hard chair
in a small room under a bare
light. They are going to get
the truth out of me if it's the
last thing they do if they must
break every bone in my body
to do it. I should be excited
but I'm not. I have rehearsed
for them before. I have seen all
of their busy knives. I am
watching them now as they
take the nails out of my fingers
slowly with aluminum pliers.
The details of torture are boring.
These are the men in black boots,
eaters of rare beef, bourbon
drinkers who smile fondly
before they break somebody's
jaw in a bar. These are fathers
of beautiful girls in soft
sweaters, men who itch at nudes
at conventions in cities they
have never been hungry in.
I do not like being naked before
them. I stammer when they ask
my name and they know they have
me. I give them the information
they want and leave for another
town on an early bus, but they
are always waiting for me at
the next station. They hold me

tight by the arms as they hustle
me into their cars from the side
doors of hotels I stay in. Finally,
too tired to love them, I walk
to the roof of a building and
jump. I am caught in a soft net
held by pairs of steel hands.

It is morning.
My mind has
fur on it
I crawl from my room
to the roof
to the ledge

and flop
head first
over the brick edges.
I fall
fast

several hundred feet
toward city stone.

I hit.
Become
four thousand red flowers
singing.

I return upstairs.
Breakfast.
I have
bacon with my coffee.

WHEN A CHILD DIES

In an empty room
with its shades pulled against the sun
the toys of our childhood
reach up for our small hands

our cribs take naps by themselves
and the bodiless voices of our mothers
tell us to sleep or that
we are late for our supper. In empty

backyards where small heels and the fat
paws of dogs have torn up the grass
a chain and an ownerless collar hang from
a wire. At night they run across the yard
looking for a neck to belong to.

Cats that know no hands
purr and rub their backs against the silence
and playwheels in empty cages
spin around and around
as if feet pounded across their tops.

The child moves strangely in the snow,
giving up love and television sets. He is
becoming an animal of motion.
The child is running away. The grownups
are calling to him, they are sorry.

He walks on, his bundle on his shoulder
ignoring their calls. Later
he is married without his father's
blessing. Later he enters a business

no one admires. He becomes rich,
fathers his own children, some of them
run away. Soon he will walk off with
a coffin, another bundle on his shoulders.

Others will call to him, He will not look back.
When he is dead they will give away
his clothing and sell his furniture. His
papers will be given to a library. Bulldozers
will be driven through his house

and a new highway will be built.
Then, in the morning. the executor of his estate
will sit over a bowl of cereal sugared
by his ashes. Will eat not knowing that
a finger of the dead man will re-form

in his throat. It will not go away. I
have to remember this every year when I bury
a friend or watch my children
climb into busses that carry them off.

I have to remember that I mocked my father
that I didn't ask my mother to
my wedding, that I stole from my
employers, that I am always sorry, that
I must watch out for unwelcome bundles

on the ridges of my shoulders.
Today I stopped answering the telephone
forever. Tomorrow I will not look back
when I hear the voices call my name.

I am working with the possibilities
of surrender: the smile of
ownership on the face of your conqueror
the little grip of the shoulder,
"Now you can stop fighting, now

you will be well-taken-care-of."
These sounds are like soft cushions
under my mind. I have the will to give in.
My generals will have to hang themselves
and my diplomats will walk up gallows

of the enemy with their wrists
manacled before them. I will learn to spell
baseball and the dead can come home
down the ramps of airplanes wearing smiles,
their hands holding tiny neckties from the grave.

When a child dies the forehead of god
should clench like an arthritic fist
and the limbs of trees should hold each
other against the dark like parting lovers.

When a child is murdered we should lead
ourselves into the forest at night
to sleep in caves, having erased the
small stones and pieces of bread that
could have led us back to one another.

I am sorry and of myself
I am sorry. It is all

you can ask it is all
you will get. My eyes

can look at your eyes. My
hands are out, palms up

and empty. Listen, if
I love you this is all

you can know of it. I can
sit with my back to you,

I can speak to you without
an answer or a question.

And when I lay the bowl at
your place you pick it up.

Oh you can drink from it fully.

I

You count up the ways you are
successful, the trophies on your
mantle, letters from men of

note, your lovely wife, the children's
grades at school. You consider
the future as if it were there, you

know the names of operas and
the stars who sing in them, the
maitre de knows your name and

favorite table, the city picks you out
in crowd scenes. It would have been
a better world if you had run for

office. But now you watch two men
in denim jackets cross your
kitchen floor, you try to move your

hamstrung legs away from knives
in their hands and the blood in
your eyes sees the blood in theirs.

II

Her eyes are blue white and look
at, not through you, her winter coat
hangs in chunks, the dugs of her
last litter are dry and tight

against her body. Each day she brings
home a new scar and the yard fills
with her prizes. A gutted woodchuck.

Deer's leg and hoof. Something. A few

feathers, a stillborn colt or fawn.
The game warden drives slowly past
our house. One day a hide full of
buckshot. At night I lie on my back

in bed, hands folded on my chest,
field mice trembling in my teeth.

III

The actors are in the kitchen.
They are busy being somebody else.

They hold their glasses as if they are mugs
and whisper about death like presidents or surgeons.
with jars of vital organs locked in their desks.

They have been everything. They have
had their shoelaces and belts removed
and been locked in concrete rooms

and had their shoes removed and been walked
smelling of urine to where cyanide waits
and the curious watch death through windows.

Now they turn to each other above the hors d'oeuvres

like spring elk charging across the table
and, knifed against the beige refrigerator

they turn, laugh, and pour each other's drinks.

IV

A witch casts a spell between commercials
in my livingroom. Machines laugh at her.
A four-year-old eats chocolate pie and watches.

She is learning magic from a sheet of glass.
She is entering the mystery on wings of air.

Outside, hungry flies grow in caves in the ground.
Wasps hum in one chimney, yellowjackets in another.

Ghosts of the Seneca dance in the torn foundation.

Yesterday I found a letter from a British regular
to his mistress, a maid in the house of rebels.
If you should never hear from me again, it said,

you can look for me in the bellies of savages.

V

It is four o'clock in the afternoon in July.
A coyote turns from the carcass of a lizard
to watch the Spaniard's horse wince as a
cactus spine invades her right front hoof.

A priest further back in the long column
runs his chubby fingers over the rosary
he will jab at the mouth of the burning

Aztec chief some weeks ahead. In the darkness
more than two thousand miles north and east
Pocohantas' grandfather rolls toward his wife.
It will be five centuries before an albino fly

crawls through the dead fish at Lake Erie
and realizes he is going to live forever.

When the light and I go out
and there's no way up from
the pool of eyes waiting for me
at the end of my day, my hands
find each other over my chest
for the little bit of warmth

they can afford. When my mind
is finished with me I fall
from it into shadows and wait
for myself, hoping I will
come back. Listen, will you

talk to me as I go out
of this, fill a hole with the
sound of us talking against
the night, unfold a hand
from the other and hold it

in your own? There is no
other way and no one else
to answer. You do not
answer either, it is your
question, my hand holding you.

for Linda Gutstein

You either had or didn't
a mother. She

loved you or not. She

neglected or might be
always there too much, a

lover. You either hated or did not

love or did
her. That is all fine.

You are well or sick by it.
Welcome then anyway.

Welcome aboard.

THE LITTLE STONES

The little stones line up on the road
and march off. Some are for windows
some are for foreheads, some for the
slipping wheels of locomotives. As they
reach their stations they turn off
without saying goodbye to each other.
This one is lucky. He will be a jewel.
He will live on the breasts of beautiful
women and in the pockets of thieves.
Now this one stops. He is meant for the
hand of a child and the eye of the child's
sister. And here is a row of four. See
how they march together? These stones
will grow large, they will signal the
tombs of a family, one for the mother
and father, one for the daughter and two
for the son who dies in a strange land.
And a handful of six round, white stones
to rub against each other in the pocket
of a mathematician. These six stones
will conjure numbers that haven't been
invented yet, will measure galaxies, the
speed of solar systems, the deaths of stars.
And the stars, exploding, will become
stones and will line up again on a road
and march off, some for windows, some for
foreheads, some for the slipping wheels
of locomotives or the tombs of families
of four—the mother, father, daughter, the
son with his body in one land, his grave
in another, each of them marked by a stone.

I

A man is found dead in his garden
or a man is not found dead in his garden

he is found on the floor of his office
over a sheaf of building plans, or
in the backseat of his car next to his

daughter's best friend, also dead, or
at the end of a knife that is reaching
for the hand that abandoned it. Perhaps

he is just found on the floor beside
his hospital bed where everybody had
expected to find him in the first place.

We have been home for a week now, the
goldenrod is ripe in the sideyard, making

my oldest daughter choke in the thick
August air. We brought the stray dog
back with us and all the lost cats returned.

The boy we hired for the summer kept the
lawn we use and the backyard mowed. We
were gone for three months. While we were gone

I learned to cook excellent spareribs, to
hit a pitched ball left-handed and to play
several Protestant hymns on my daughters'

guitars. I started smoking again and lost
about thirty pounds. It is probably true
that a man is never found dead, that

he gets away before we discover him and
that this handful of flowers is lying on
ground as empty as the hand that dropped them.

It is also probably true that this isn't water
we are pouring on a mound of sod and grass
but a voice we went to sleep to, harmonizing

with a handsaw when we were small enough
to fall asleep on one end of a worktable
with our father working at the other end.

II

The leaves sound like rain in the wind.
The ground spiders tie things together.
The corpse of a small thing catches my eye
at the edge of the yard. I walk to it,
a rat's body without a head, victim of
one of the dogs, it is nothing I want.
One dog sleeps by the wooden bench I
sit down on, the wood table I work at.
A car speeds past the edge of my sight
and a school bus takes its place on the
tar road. My smallest daughter's legs fall
into view on the far side. A door shuts.
She runs to me dressed in red and blue wool.

III

He is taller than his father.
This pleases him and doesn't bother the old man.
Together they sit in the bleachers
behind third base

(which is the son's position)

rather than the catcher (his father's years before)

and watch the baseman, George Kell
a man with a name much like theirs

(Kelly)

which is probably why the boy chose that position
to play on his own team, a neighborhood team
made up of boys from the ages of ten to fourteen

and wearing white polo shirts with the legend

McWILLIAMS STORES

across the chest and numbers on the back.
The father is smoking a large, inexpensive cigar

and leans over from the waist
from time to time to spit
down between the bleachers.

He explains to his son that
although he enjoys a cigar
once in awhile he can only
smoke them outdoors as they make him have to spit

so much.

At other intervals during the game
the father smokes handrolled, Bull Durham cigarettes.

The scores, chronologically, in the game are

0-0
then
1-0

then
2-1
2-2
4-2
and finally 5-2.

After the game they walk home
through the stadium neighborhood
with a stop at a tavern

where the father has beer and a shot of whiskey
and the boy has a glass of Coke. When they get home

they walk in through the front door
and past the livingroom
where the mother is sitting

mending a sock. She asks them
if they had a good time
and they both answer yes.

She thinks they are probably telling the truth.

                    IV

This is my year, the year of the tiger.
Twelve years ago I took my first job, and
twelve years before I entered high school.
This year I will go into a convent with
old meat stinking on my breath. I will
embrace the faith, eat wafers, rape nuns.
David you are entering a new life, they will
say to me, and to each other, do you see
how they all come back at last? My mother

will be pleased in Florida, she will take
off her sunglasses for the first time in days
and my father will be warmer in his grave
a half-mile back from Eastern avenue. The
relatives will all line up in their family
rooms, their offices, their coffins. Do
you remember when he entered high school?
Do you remember his first job or how red
he was in the delivery room? And I will walk
through the butterflies of applause, my thumb
over the rim of my martini glass, waiting
for 1986, the ice-age, my new saber teeth.

V

We accumulate a life, begin with
a person, a pet bird, a house perhaps
some simple furniture, let it be
of wood, the walls will be too

and you will be dressed in wool
and other simple things, some
leather for the feet, some cotton

the one extravagance a ring made
from gold and topaz—but not a precious
stone and not too well-made either

and then a crude mat of straw for your head.

Now. Let us put you in your garden
a rich place in which you let weeds grow
as well as flowers, your hat pushed back
to wipe sweat from your forehead, trowel
dripping dirt in your right hand, and

the promise of flowers bright in your eye.

In the stove inside, a wood fire waits, at
this page a poet is beginning to know you.

For Frank Lima

Some days I think I should be in the basement
                    inventing the machinegun
for the second time or sharpening both sides of my
                       machete on a lathe.
Some days I sit in my room until sundown, rubbing
                     poems like garlic
on the filed tips of bullets meant for werewolves,
                   generals and priests.

Some nights I crawl through the side doors of bars
                    like a starving rat
just to smell the songs oozing like cheese from the
                    drinkers' pores
and some nights, the ones before my birthdays, I sleep
                    with eyes open
until the light comes back and old women hurry out
                  to sweep the streets.

Midnight.
There are eight small motors

outside, whirling around each other on the snow
close to the window, their headlights

passing over the bed
and then they are gone.

A fly buzzes itself to death on the floor beside me.
My fingers look for something in my hair.

An hour goes by
and then another

and a third follows them.
A dog screams the moon

and another answers back
and you shift and whimper beside me

under your blanket
and my mouth tastes like the dead

and I am sorry for everything
and my tongue peels

against my teeth
and the two kittens

playing downstairs bang the house
against the edges of the night

and if this is me, I whisper,
please give it one more chance.

For Cynthia

I

Tomorrow's suicides walk slowly down long flights
of stairs;
their fingers are always caressing the edges of things.

II

Van Gogh walks into an afternoon of bright colored
birds;
the field of wheat has turned black, the birds are
yellow.

III

Sometimes a suicide wants to call for help but not too
successfully;
she takes the pills, gets on the phone, calls her most
inept friend.

IV

He got tired of listening to the noises the house made
at night;
when he made them go away his life got up and
walked out with them.

V

Finally you have the chair and the rope in their
proper places;
your last act is to lock the door to your room from
the outside.

A crow waits in the top of a tree
for the raccoon to leave its dead mate
in the road. The bird shifts a claw
on its branch and chestnuts fall.
I am at a window on the third floor
of an old house. I have just read
a poem I wrote ten years ago. I like it.
In town only the old men on street
corners discuss the history of spring.
Downstairs in the master bedroom
my wife and youngest daughter sleep.
One flight further down the television
kills two hours until the evening news.
It is the Lenten season, as it has been
thirty-four other times in my life
and I am still not Catholic. Ten years
ago I was without hope. Now I am hopeless.
Even my mother has given up wringing
her hands when she sees me, even
my employers are tired of shaking their
heads. Listen. Today, washing my hair
in the bathtub, I got shampoo in
my eyes. For ten minutes the pain
was more important than all your wars.
Or this. My daughter, up from her nap
has tiptoed up the stairs and, still
a little sleepy, is tugging at the
edges of my sweater as I stand here.
Her hands are the smallest in the world.

The wind is cold
in a clean glass.
I lie outdoors
on an old couch
drinking and you
move the silence
as you walk past.

Baby trots by
on tiptoes.
Little pig feet
my hairy chin
chin
the fat peach
cheek
of her. Last
night
we
gave her rum
to sleep by
fast asleep.
But
trot right by
on pink pig toes.
A grape
her moon full face
cracks wide.
Impossible face of
smile.
Nice.
Her nice is nice.

I wake up in the morning, the room filled
with photographs of old friends, boats leaving,
signed confessions and the sighs of animals
informed they were born to appear one day
as the entrees on some politician's menu. A friend

has died in a plane, she is all the metal that a hill
in Wisconsin can hold. Pitchforks and flashlights
pry into piles of straw for her soul, dogs tug at
                                        leashes.

Another day more or less and you would be here with
                                        us now
instead of this empty chair, this coffee mug
with your name on it. I am waiting for you to come
                                        home.

Since you left the backyard plays by itself,
the dog sleeps all day, the new car runs but only
in reverse, its keys not fitting anything.
The piano against the dining room wall hums to
                                        itself.
I come near it and it stops. There should be a picture

here, over my desk, of your eyes smiling out
from something we did together in the past. Instead
I have nailed the room to its own mantel. I gaze
at it every day. Was the last sound you listened to
an owl breaking mice? Or was it the song the moon
makes over fields when the living aren't there?

Empty busses pass the house at dawn and dark
their useless doors sighing like condemned men.
In the evenings I lie on my back and imagine

the mice playing in the attic. When you come back
I will buy a cat. You will love it and it will love
                                        mice

Now I wake up like everyone else, with my teeth
and my soul coated with scum and with the shades
                                        drawn
and with no knowledge of where I am. Like everyone
                                        else
I ring for service and I give the desk my name
and a porter brings up my life on a breakfast tray.

And I tip him and he forgets to thank me.
And I wonder which of us has given and how much.

WOLVES OF NORTH AMERICA

for Janis Cohen

Ray Godlewski is real.
Barnaby Phobbs I made up.
Angelica Withers probably exists
somewhere. We love
the names of things we

avoid abstractions.
We love painfully
and with finite care.
Our voices are ponderous.

It is the end of something,
a decade perhaps
an era maybe a
race

a species. I make up
Barnaby Phobbs because
I am afraid I
love you and
I am afraid.

The moon-halved house
slips white fingers
through shadows at night.

While frogs cry
I hide on the dark side

looking in
at an empty piano
someone has left behind.

How long has it been?
I dug a shallow hole
into the front yard

while branches of the black elm
tore at my hair.

How long has it been
since the blind dog moaned
while I crashed the rusted shovel
into hollow crematory boxes

into your waiting
burned bones?

This is the beginning of the first page of a diary:
"Today I am going to Sioux Falls with Leon."
That morning she was killed in a small car beneath a
                                        truck.
It rained that morning and a pope was ill and the
                                        Braves lost
but the important facts were about Sioux Falls and Leon
and that she was going there with him or that she and he
were going somewhere and that she was beginning a
                                        diary
that would end on the same page and day she began it.
The important facts to the State Police were the skid
                                        marks
measured along a wet road and from lane to lane and
                                        recorded.
To a truck driver from Cleveland, Ohio, the importance
lay in the number of crushed ribs the X-rays would
                                        show
and whether or not his chauffeur's license would be
                                        revoked
and if it was then how he would pay the room and
                                        board
of a youngest son locked in a home for the moronic
and what to do with a house he'd never been able to
afford and a nervous wife who had trouble sleeping
                                        nights.
In Cleveland the wife was busy with the neighbors' son
home from college and beside her in bed for the week.
She hoped she'd be able to get him out of it before the
neighborhood came awake and the cleaning lady came
                                        for
the day. He was still asleep when the telephone rang.
The gum chewing girl who connected the call had been

worried all week about a boy friend who was
                                    standing now
since dawn in the mud in a camp in Georgia and who
                                    hadn't
answered the letter that told him what the doctor had
                                    said
because he was busy with a fat sergeant with
                                    heartburn. She
disconnected the call before the nervous wife learned
                                    that
her husband was not dead. And the cleaning lady,
                                    troubled
in mind by an oldest son whose income depended on
                                    the earnings
of two young girls in hotels in Cleveland came up the
walk, heard a scream and saw a frightened college kid
break through the door and flash by her across the
                                    damp
lawn with his clothes half on and vanish into the
                                    house
next door. A nurse walked into an Iowa hospital
                                    room with
a syringe filled with dolophine. Two sets of Iowa
                                    parents,
still a little sleepy, looked at two young faces under
lifted sheets in two rooms in the emergency ward.
                                    And
a young reporter from a bankrupt small town paper
                                    opened
a book he'd found on the wet road and read the first
                                    lines:
"Today I am going to Sioux Falls with Leon."

When the generals break for coffee the war ends for
                                ten minutes.
The sounds of children exploding vanish into a break
                               in the clouds
and the oxen turn from their flaming hides to the cuds
                               in their
mouths, their owners' feet point earthwards again
                             and follow plows.

When the generals break for coffee the planet Mars
                             turns soft blue
and angels sitting on the points of stars break out
                             their harps
while choirs of the dead serenade the planet for ten
                             minutes.

The horse lies on his side
in the barnyard next to the
dirt drive, his forelegs
crossed. His eyes are half
opened and he drags his head
up from the ground as the
red pickup grows larger on
the road and stops big in
the dirt beside him. My uncle
swings open the truck door
and gets out. Tall. Thin.
Black hair and half drunk.
He walks to the horse, kneels
by it and looks in its eyes.
The horse wheezes, tries to
get up. My uncle stands,
walks back to the truck, opens
the door on the rider's side
and gets his gun out of the
glove compartment. A revolver.
Black beside the whiskey bottle.
He lifts the safety and walks
back to the horse. My uncle
is underweight. His wife cries
sometimes in the night. He
kneels back by the horse and
pats its nose. Sticks the
barrel behind an ear. The shot
is less loud than you'd expect.
Then the farmer comes out
of his house and helps us
load the body on the truck.

Picture a valley of dry grass
and yourself on the rim of it
looking down to the center

where you see, standing, its
large shaggy head mowing the
ground with the breath from

its nostrils, a buffalo, a bull
and very old but huge in size
and of a certain greatness.

Sitting around him in a half
circle, leaning forward from
their haunches are seven gray

wolves, buffalo wolves the
settlers call them because of
the meat they seem to favor.

All eight of the animals are
out of breath and face each
other without violence now

and the distance between the
bull and the teeth that face
him remains nearly the same

for several minutes. Picture
the sun very high and bright
and a nervous horse under you.

The rough hair on the buffalo's
head is filled with burrs, his
tongue hangs black from his mouth

and his hooves paw the ground
before him. The wolves pant,
return their tongues into

their mouths and nose each
other, whimpering and snarling
as they squat, rise, turn

and shift not far from their
enemy's head. Three of them
are patched with mange, five

are males, two females. Imagine
now that your horse whinnies
in fear and turns in a circle

and you barely hear another
noise coming from the scene
below you. When you've settled

your horse you think it was
a groan from the trapped bull
but you're not sure because

it was drowned out again immediately
by a chorus of howls from the
wolves. Then you hear it again

but much louder and again the
cadenced howls and your horse
trembles beneath your legs.

Imagine that these animals still
have hardly moved in relation
to each other and that as you

hear the bull for the third
time, and this is a bellow

louder than any noise you've

ever heard from such a dis-
tance, a lone cloud passes
across the sun and the valley

becomes gray and dark as the
whole seven wolves answer the
bull with a long, low wail.

And hear the cry of each of
these eight beasts flowing
back and forth between each

other and the deep brass sound
of the bull controlling the
pace of the others and listen

as you wheel your horse around
and leave in the other direction
from this meeting to the sudden

hush in this chorus and to
what you know, even though
the center of the valley is

at least a half mile from you
and you probably can't really
hear it are the slick and much

quieter percussions as they
whisk over each other of
seven sets of very expert teeth.

Sport, the

bird falling from the peak of its arc, the
dog landing on the spent fox, the

motorcycle
failing to cross
the full space

the fire dropping on the pony's back

prizefighters stumbling through old gymnasiums
their mops erasing blood clots from the floors

the crack of a bat

and they're off. They're off.

FILMING ASSASSINATIONS

The door opens and someone always steps out on
                              the film. It
isn't always the right man; sometimes you have to
                              wait until
near the end for the gun and camera to focus on the
                              proper tar-
get, for unreal blood to fall on the concrete. But in
                              truth,
anyplace will do and any method. A window opens
                              at the wrong
time and a man and rifle on a roof that has been
                              waiting for
years become a moment in history. A convertible top
                              is left
down and the flow of traffic on a certain street will
                              always
run in the opposite direction. Or a hand somewhere
                              in a friendly
crowd reaches through two bees that need a heart to
                              sing in.
And in any case the film always snaps, becomes drunk
                              and out
of focus or was concentrating on an attendant door,
                              the door
no one is ever seen coming out of.

I

When the water runs out it is because someone leaves
                                        the
tap running. I tell her this and the next day we're
                                        out of
water again. This is not unusual. The only time she
                                        ever lets
the dog out is when it's in heat, the only time the
                                        door is
closed is in summer when the screens are up and it's
                                        hot.
Sometimes she sighs loudly while we make love.

II

He is under orders. He moves with a sense of purpose.
                                        He wears
his hands in fists at his sides. He is a uniform. His
                                        eyes
glint with the steel of conviction. To him, the
                                        world is a
target.

But wait. Let's make this more personal. You are
                                        his target.
You always will be. You are his purpose. Be proud
                                        as he shoulders
you and strides toward the flames like a truck. Be
                                        glad you
are his aide, the partner you could never die without.

III

We are closing up. In the farmyard the last turkey
has been
assigned to the last pilgrim, the last egg to the last
fox,
the last bull to the last matador. Back inside the
tent the
trapeze girls are throwing dice for the love of the
peanut
vendor, the lion has eaten his trainer and given
himself up
to the moths. This is my last meal and your last
poem.

IV

But what is it I was lying about before I was
interrupted?
Churchyards? Old lovers? The staleness of draught
beer in a
particular town? Perhaps it was an anecdote,
beginning, "They
came for him at dawn."

V

Finally it comes down to this. They were both
cremated, one of
them fourteen years before the other. His ashes were
saved
the whole time until hers were ready.

They were going to be buried together under the giant

                                        black wal-
nut tree but it had been sold for lumber by then. If
                                        the boats
had been running they could have been spread into
                                        the sea, but
they were put into the sand along the shore instead.

People I know are always approaching me
with the threat they are going to break.

This threat has an odor, it is of old
orange peels and Panamanian grass. It is also
where the moon breaks in two and offers

to puncture your eyeballs. Wait. I am too loud here.

Let me try again.

I'll call her Marlene because
I like the name and don't know anyone
who uses it.

She is wrapped around herself in the center
of an overstuffed chair. Call it her father

if you like or even call it death.

Or the book I am holding in my lap.
Her book of songs. "This is my book of songs,"
she says. "I have no one to sing them."

I tell her to sing them herself.

"I never had a child of my own," she says,
"and now I am afraid that I have cancer."

You are a judge and it is Friday
and you are a day late. They have hanged the wrong
man.
This year your nasturtiums will be caught
by a late frost and your investments will decline.
Your four-year-old son vomits when you
try to feed him his cereal. When you
take walks after supper you are followed by
the strident voices of journalists. Your advisors
will suggest a new brand of fertilizer, the
spring rains will gall your peaches.
Your credit has been stopped at the grocer's and
your maid refuses to dust the portrait of your father.
When you wake up each morning it is still dark
outside and when you come home at night
a red sun is just beginning to rise. You
sit out on the porch with your friends, drinking
to their futures and they fail to give back
your toasts. Your election has been won, already
the first apology begins to stink on your lips.
What you say is of no importance; you
cannot change the colors of a dying field
or the song of the flesh-eating horse
before he falls upon a captive's throat. You cannot
stay an execution by going there, a letter
of confession in your fist, you cannot hold back a curtain
after the actors have given in to their fear
and collapsed, weeping into each other's arms and,
when grim men, their teeth clenched
like bars on a cell door reach your house in the night
their hands calling your name against wood
you can show them no further credentials.
You must give in and be their leader and your victim.

Friday afternoon and the rain
slides down empty windows.
I am wet on your gray streets,
stabbed by family lighted houses.

I remember the girl from another time,
smiling and dressed for another season;
now she is turning in the dim lights.
Each night she follows the strangers home.

These are your streets and your corners;
this is the starched sky, the prim skirt
that hides you from year to year,
muffling the odor of your real songs.

In Peru the indians chew betel,
walk through thin brown streets,
stand in the high market squares
with mad thoughts crawling their backs.

The sun is down the streetlights are on;
sidewalks run home whining in fear.
Only the wounded are left in the rain.
Soon the quiet wagons will arrive for them.

I am afraid since
you had the last baby

of your pain
spilling over my magazine pages
your blood on my hands

on a steering wheel
or the doctor

walking into the waiting room
with his stained gloves

and unreadable face.

Winter is coming again, an old nun
loaded down with frozen groceries. Suicides
turn from their lives like the minds
of automobile drivers avoiding gutted dogs
they have driven over on the roads
before dinner, and cigarette smokers
who thought they had quit are back in line
at the tobacco counters, changing brands.
Winter is moving in from the horizon
and the killers of deer are buying new coats.
Fat gray bears, stupid and slow are being
informed they have had their paroles revoked.
The old man who sells us fuel is smiling
for the first time since June, blackbirds
eat the last of the wild grapes outside.
Soon they will beat their huge wings
against our windows, begging the table scraps
we'll have fed to our cats and the snow will
be punctuated by their dark, starved bodies.
In the mornings that are just like night
we will rummage through the empty bottles
on the tables for matches, for prayer books and gloves
and at night we will lie against each other
our fingers stiff as corpses seeking warmth.
We will celebrate the birth of an old god
the death of a new year, the endless killing of time
and when spring comes we will all be older
and we will spill out our doors like drunken
cripples. We will plan trips to the shore
to watch fish breaking free of the ice,
to watch gulls feeding, our children playing

on the sand where we will try to plant corn,
our winter blankets fading in the sun.
And the children will wonder why, even at noon
and even in August we grope for these blankets, why
shivering we still wrap them around ourselves.

A BACKYARD FOR THE DEAD TO REST IN

Somewhere on a manicured street
a poem is waiting, poised behind a lace curtain
only its gloved right hand showing
as it pulls the cloth aside a moment
in order to check the progress of blossoms
on a neighborhood's cherry tree
on Fancher Street in Mt. Pleasant, Michigan
years before any of you died or even
clutched a diseased stomach, back
when pain was as simple as a baseball my father
threw too hard in my aunt and uncle's
backyard, into my gloved hand
that peers now through a poem, through curtains
and into a manicured street to check
cherry trees in a backyard where
the dead can come and rest a moment.

I am looking out a wide window at
a quarter mile of land covered with snow
and thinking about someone who has been
in the ground for over a year. The war is over

and the dead can come home now, walking
down the ramps of airplanes, wearing
smiles, their hands holding little neckties

from the grave. How was it where you were,
we will ask, crowding around the empty boxes
they will pull on chains behind them. They
will tell us there was never anything
to worry about, they were home all along

that it is we who have come home at last.
And we will laugh at this together, the dead
and the living. And those who do not under-
stand the joke will explain it to those who do.

We can't pretend any longer, our resources
are expended, ammunition gone, all the men
are dead. These figures around us are

not white. We are on our knees, bleeding,
reading our reflections in a bend of the
Little Big Horn. They say Custer you have not
come home; in another century tourists will

pass here on a bus, cameras pointing at your death.
At lunch they will argue the name of your horse.

It is four hours after sundown.
The dogs are full, they have had meat
and they cannot feel that night crawls
under the door and through all the windows.

I reach my hand into an empty space.
It is taken but by nothing warm.
There is a room, someone is singing.
I move through a crowd asking the time.

I meet you in a dark room where it
is raining. If you smile I can't see it.
I turn up your collar for you.
Give me your hand. Give me your hand.

All right, spring is finally here.
I am in the north with my children, my
promises. It is April and the snow stays
and here I am in the field, naked

lying again on chilled ground. I am
viewed from above as through clouds,
the headlines behind my eyes lighting the way.

All day long
I have been contemplating my right hand.

This is the one that can play
half a piano better than the other
the one that turns a doorknob fastest

the one that gives and takes away.

I have also been watching
the cars go by
on the road outside, dozens of them
buzzing past. One
of them stopped. I didn't answer the door

and it went back somewhere I
assume. I tried to nap

but couldn't sleep, tried to work and felt guilty.

All day long
I have been trying only a little
to do something, travelling

from the last drink last night
to the first one tonight
with incredible ease. Then

I will sit drunken before strangers
who ignore me on the television screen. I
will laugh and tell them the names

and addresses I don't hear from anymore
and they will ignore me but I won't turn them off.
In the cold hour before dawn
I am writing my will. I leave myself to myself.

I am no longer negotiable. My
diplomats have gone home. Rumors of bombs
fall on the streets. Communications lines

are down. Last night I woke in the dark
and heard the trees scream
as they crawled over the ground, limbs breaking,
their many hands reaching out for many hands.

Inside I sit by the large radio
waiting for news from the front
and warming my hands at an old fire.

They are all I have. The woman and the children
sleeping in the rooms upstairs
don't know me anymore and the rooms go empty
each time I look along them for a face.

Beautiful, you say, your last days wrapped in smiles.
Your thoughts wait in a closet like uniforms
from an old war. Your fingers reach for their gun.

In alleys behind the old taverns
people replace the cats in the trash
and the shadows of ghosts bow to each other.

Let me alone in this cave in the back of my mind
with your voice floating out like smoke from a hole
                              at the top.
Walk out the door with your hands in front of you,
your memories of me an emptiness in your flexed
                              wrist and
the cold silence of a room even loneliness has aban-
                              doned.

I have been lying on the same spot on this bed for
                              three days,
my eyes open and voices from the hall outside asking,
"When will he return? Will his feet burn a hole in
                              the floor?"
But I am going now and I do not want you to watch
                              me
as my bare hands curl at my sides and my legs curl
                              like iguanas.

After the fear has gone and the night follows it
even the echo of my footsteps will ring like the bells
sounding for a dawn in which you have no place to
                              rest
and where only we who have left you behind will
                              see light.

Afternoons in Geneseo
trying to claw poems out of the ground
like winter potatoes. An
occasional shot, somebody is killing
birds. A family of pheasants

builds nests in our grapevines. The
phone rings, a delivery of oil arrives,
the dog barks. We tell the hunters
they can't come into our fields
and they walk off laughing
something about my beard, my wife's dress.

Centuries ago we closed our gills
and grew lungs and looked up at
the roof of the sea for the last time.
This afternoon it rains as I
read the news and feel homesickness
close over my head like a fresh sheet.

I go back to the typewriter.
A yellow bus comes, a child gets off.
It is Geneseo, it is afternoon.
If I were in Lisbon I'd be
doing more than this, if I
were in Moscow, in London, less.

Less than this table spread
with paper, the smell of pheasant
cooking downstairs. Wherever you are
it is at somebody else's throat.
Whoever it is, it is yours.

The new coffee is marvelous.
Thousands dance in the streets, cheering, singing
and the doors to the prisons are opened,
pardons handed out, condemned men freed.
The new coffee is delicious, cancers remit
from bodies that had despaired, clouds
dissipate, the air is clean and sweet
as the breath of angels. The new coffee
is a wonder, canyons close and the
wind blows the odor of roses
into sewers, thin brown rats grow
ribbons of gold and pink, raise themselves
on their hind legs and tiptoe the streets
playing lightly on wooden flutes.
The new coffee is a wonder,
the new coffee moves us all to ecstasy
and underneath the icebergs
in the darkest caves of water, the songs
of cold blue whales, contralto and round
as the birth of mystery begin their slow journey
through the oceans to our waiting ears.

It is good Friday.
In town the Christians are recreating their old
                                            disaster.
My two oldest daughters play
and holler in the yard out back. The
youngest coughs steadily in her bedroom down the
                                                hall.

She will wake up and want to play outside.

The sky at the rim of the valley twenty miles west
                                                of us
wears its usual ring of brown air. The East has not
                                                been

evacuated yet. Twice a year
Canadian geese cry down as you walk
in to the house from the car.

I heard them again this morning.

It is one disaster
or another, the

burning of a house, a president's
assassination, a friend's
divorce, the death of a babysitter's father.

Some colleagues have been fired.
An earthquake has decimated a city.
A pretty woman has been told she is inoperable

and a heavy man whose wife and children love him
                                                desperately

has turned gray and crashed into the ground.
He will need expensive burying.

In town people are dressed in mourning. A month
                                                    ago

they smeared themselves with ashes. Today
I look out through the sunlight and watch a hawk

rise out of the grass
with a rabbit in its claws. In

less than a minute it vanishes, flying higher and
                                        quicker

than a man on this day
can ever hope to see.